Lecture Notes in Computer Science 578

Edited by G. Goos and J. Hartmanis

Advisory Board: W. Brauer   D. Gries   J. Sto

Th. Beth   M. Frisch   G. J. Simmons (Eds.)

Public-Key Cryptography: State of the Art and Future Directions

E.I. S. S.Workshop
Oberwolfach, Germany, July 3–6, 1991
Final Report

Springer-Verlag
Berlin Heidelberg New York
London Paris Tokyo
Hong Kong Barcelona
Budapest

Series Editors

Gerhard Goos
Universität Karlsruhe
Postfach 69 80
Vincenz-Priessnitz-Straße 1
W-7500 Karlsruhe, FRG

Juris Hartmanis
Department of Computer Science
Cornell University
5148 Upson Hall
Ithaca, NY 14853, USA

Volume Editors

Thomas Beth
Markus Frisch
European Institute for System Security (E.I.S.S.), Universität Karlsruhe
Am Fasanengarten 5, W-7500 Karlsruhe, FRG

Gustavus J. Simmons
National Security Studies, SANDIA National Laboratories
P. O. Box 5800, Org. 700, Albuquerque, NM 87185, USA

OOS·82 BET

CR Subject Classification (1991): E.3, F.2.1

ISBN 3-540-55215-4 Springer-Verlag Berlin Heidelberg New York
ISBN 0-387-55215-4 Springer-Verlag New York Berlin Heidelberg

© Springer-Verlag Berlin Heidelberg 1992
Printed in Germany

Typesetting: Camera ready by author
Printing and binding: Druckhaus Beltz, Hemsbach/Bergstr.
45/3140-543210 - Printed on acid-free paper

92 0695612

Preface

The "European Institute for System Security (E.I.S.S.)" was founded on February 29, 1988 by cabinet resolution of the state government Baden-Württemberg. It is headed by Professor Thomas Beth and is affiliated with the Institute for Algorithms and Cognitive Systems (IAKS) of the Faculty for Computer Science at the University of Karlsruhe (TH). From November 1, 1988 to November 30, 1990, the institute was situated in the rooms of the building Kaiserstrasse 8 (title picture annual report 1988/89) on the campus of the University of Karlsruhe. Even back then, the E.I.S.S. was provided with a seminar and conference room, laboratory and computer rooms as well as a separate administration office and a library, apart from rooms for the permanently employed staff and visiting scientists.

Since December 1, 1990, the E.I.S.S. is situated together with the Institute for Algorithms and Cognitive Systems in the new building of the Faculty for Computer Science, Am Fasanengarten 5.

In accordance with the cabinet resolution, the basic task setting for the E.I.S.S. is scientific research and knowledge transfer in the field of security in telecommunications, computer and information systems. These tasks are dealt with in the scope of European projects and in cooperation with other private and public research institutions.

Among the E.I.S.S. tasks are mainly

- Research and development projects in the field of data security technology for open networks,

- Research and development projects in the field of data security technology in information and computer systems,

- Procurement and evaluation of up-to-date research and project information within the competence of the E.I.S.S.,

- Vocational and advanced training measures in the fields of data security and security of open networks as well as of information and computer systems.

With the installation of the E.I.S.S. a centre, where the sufficient concentration of personnel, expertise and equipment is available permanently, will be dedicated in Europe to the key sector of system security, which is important for the future of information technology. Thus the core for an attractive institute has been created, where research and development, as well as knowledge transfer between science, economy and administration in Europe can be advanced.

E.I.S.S. Karlsruhe   Thomas Beth

December 1991

What Is Achieved Through this Report?

In accordance with its main task, the E.I.S.S. has convened assessment workshops on central questions of system security such as

- Open and secure information systems,

- Block cipher technology,

- Stream cipher technology and

- Security for object-oriented systems / databases.

In this suite the most recent one addressed the topic of public-key cryptography and will be followed by a workshop on state of the art of hash functions in early 1992. This report on the state of the art and future direction of public-key cryptography is made public in accordance with the terms of reference of the E.I.S.S. The publication through the Lecture Notes in Computer Science series has been chosen as a fast and cost-effective way of disseminating the results of this workshop and the know-how compiled by the invited experts to all members of the general computer science community: systems developers, researchers, decision makers, standardization committees, patent offices, and, last but not least, users and customers of secure computer systems.

Contents

1 Introduction

This is the report on "Public-Key Cryptography: State of the Art and Future Direction" describing the proceedings and discussions of the workshop organized by the European Institute for System Security in July 1992.

1.1 Historical Remarks

The central role of public-key cryptography has been recognized immediately after its discovery in the late 1970's. Several public-key cryptosystems have been proposed since. The research in computer science and mathematics have been influenced by the invention of this breakthrough during the last 15 years. Research into the security systems has not only brought deeper insights into the areas of protocol design and verification but has also stimulated and intensified research in algebra and number theory especially in the area of integer factorisation. New integer factorisation methods have been developed in almost biannual regularity, reducing complexity of factorisation to an order of magnitude which makes it today feasible to factorise numbers in a days time, which had been originally considered as safe integers in the beginning 1980's. Another output has been the research into the arithmetic for long integers challenged by the need for high speed public-key encryption. Through the invention of the public-key concept new fields have been made accessible which had not been thought of until the late 1970's. These are:

- Remote Login Protocols

- Shared Control Schemes

- Democratic Voting Schemes

- Authenticated Distributed Computing

- Electronic Money

- Distributed Management of Data Bases

Although most of these concepts have been known for more than a decade, the availability of products has not kept pace with the scientific development. Not even conventions for the basic schemes such as signatures and key exchange had been agreed upon in form of standards or common interfaces until the mid of 1991.

In view of these recent scientific, technological and political developments around public-key systems and their future use as a primitive for secure data-processing on a world wide scale, the *European Institute for System Security (E.I.S.S.)* has convened a workshop to assess the State of the Art and Future Direction of Public-Key Cryptography. This complies with the institute's mission (given by the state

government of Baden-Württemberg) to provide *know-how* compilation
and technology transfer at top scientific level to authorities, industry
and public and research communities in Germany, Europe and to the
high-tech community worldwide.

In view of the ongoing discussions on the choice of one or the other
public-key schemes which had arrived at a level of "a holy war" in
some instances, it was a natural matter for the E.I.S.S. to act as a
international platform to clarify the situation.

1.2   Who Has Contributed?

The task of assessing the present state of public-key technology to be
carried out in a balanced manner has afforded planning and careful
discussions between the world's leading experts to compose a suitable
list of invitees. Prime requirement for every invitee has been the ability
to contribute at least to 2 special topics of cryptography rather than
representing one view. Another prime requirement applied to invitees
of E.I.S.S.-workshops at this level is that every participant is active in
front line research at technological level.

Unlike most scientific meetings, this meant that the attendees at
this workshop needed to be prime movers in the field and currently
at the forefront of one or more important areas of research and development to insure that the status and projections of future direction

would be as reliable as possible.

To this report all participants of the meeting have been giving
one talk during the workshop participating in the ongoing discussions
and finally contributing to review processes in the work. The list of
participants active in these process is:

- Thomas Beth, Europäisches Institut für Systemsicherheit, Universität Karlsruhe, Germany

- Albrecht Beutelspacher, Universität Gießen, Mathematisches Institut, Germany

- James H. Davenport, School of Mathematical Sciences, University of Bath, GB

- Yvo Desmedt, University of Wisconsin – Milwaukee, Department of Electrical Engineering and Computer Science, WI, USA

- Whitfield Diffie, Sun Microsystems, Mountain View, CA, USA

- Arjen K. Lenstra, Bellcore, Morristown, NJ, USA

- Hendrik W. Lenstra, Jr., Institute for Advanced Study, Princeton, NJ, USA

- Kevin S. McCurley, Sandia National Laboratories, Division 1423, Albuquerque, NM, USA

- Peter L. Montgomery, University of California, Department of Mathematics, Los Angeles, CA, USA

- Andrew M. Odlyzko, AT&T Bell Laboratories, Murray Hill, NJ, USA

- Jean-Jacques Quisquater, Philips Research Laboratory, Louvain-la-Neuve, Belgium

- Ronald L. Rivest, MIT, Laboratory for Computer Science, Cambridge, MA, USA

- Claus P. Schnorr, Universität Frankfurt, Fachbereich Mathematik, Frankfurt am Main, Germany

- Robert D. Silverman, The MITRE Corporation, Bedford, MA, USA

- Gustavus J. Simmons, Sandia National Laboratories, Albuquerque, NM, USA

- Scott A. Vanstone, Department of Combinatorics and Optimization, University of Waterloo, Ontario, Canada

Unfortunately, out of these Kevin S. McCurley, Jean-Jacques Quisquater, Ronald L. Rivest and Scott A. Vanstone could not make it to be present in the meeting. I am most grateful for their contributions to this final report, which was written, based on the notes and contributions, prepared by the four rapporteurs:

- Markus Frisch,

- Willi Geiselmann,

- Hans-Joachim Knobloch and

- Frank Schaefer,

who as E.I.S.S. scientists did marvelous job in compiling the material and combining the topics to be addressed in the consequent chapters.

The scientific importance and independence of the workshop is indicated by the happy circumstance that it could take place at the renowned *Mathematisches Forschungsinstitut* at Oberwolfach, providing its unique facilities and surroundings for intensive research activities and communications for invited visitors from around the whole world.

1.3   Who Should Read this Report?

Although this report has been compiled by a dozen of the few world's leading experts of the field it is addressing the general computing community at all levels. The rather demanding task of writing a report which stretches from a survey like presentation enabling the non-specialist to identify the essentials of his interest, to scientific information referenced to the original literature, could only have been achieved through the very good cooperation of all participants during the meeting and after the meeting, when this text was compiled in several processes of rewriting.

The report is aimed at all members of the computing community around the world, including those who are not visiting one of the regular Cryptology and Computer Security conferences that take place annually. This report may give a brief introduction to the range of problems that could be incurred with the methods of public-key cryptography if taken as an allround remedy for all problems of computer and communications security. We address the availability of mechanisms, the cautions to be taken and the difficulties arising from the use of public-key cryptography in practical systems. In total — with all modesty — this report tries to emphasize the strength of these mechanisms and balances it versus their weaknesses and vulnerabilities. Especially the professional view expressed by all participants to look at these as sometimes expensive tools of modern authentication and security technology with some care makes it worth while reading for any one in government, offices, standardization bodies, banking and computer and telecommunications industries.

In spite of the wide range addressed the text is aiming also at all those who are at research level in cryptology, network security, computer science or mathematics to indicate the state of the art as it represents itself at the end of the one and a half decade period after invention of public-key cryptography.

1.4   Notice

The topicality of the development in this field was best demonstrated to all participants by the fact that just 5 days before the meeting the *DSS* U.S. digital signature standard [79] by the NIST (National Institute of Standards and Technology) has been announced through testimony on June 27, 1991, before the Subcommittee on Technology and Competitiveness of the U.S. House of Representatives by NIST Deputy Director Raymond G. Kammer

This development on the political side provided even more evidence for the necessity of having such a survey available for the general community by an independent body of research and technology representatives. By this the terms of reference of this meeting had even been more emphasized.

The scientific importance of this meeting may best be demonstrated by the discovery of a possibly new trapdoor to the discrete logarithm at the E.I.S.S.-workshop. This in the meantime has been brought to the attention of the public by Stuart Haber and Arjen K. Lenstra in a letter commenting the "Proposed Digital Signature Standard", published in the Federal Register on August 30, 1991.

We therefore address this report, being the summary of the essential achievements of this workshop, to all institutions, companies and organisations whose future decisions for security, methods, technology and products will certainly be influenced by the information gathered here.

I hope that therefore this report will be welcomed by the high-tech community around the world. The publication through Springer enabled us to reach the community in an open way. I am especially indebted to the Editor-in-Chief of Lecture Notes in Computer Science for himself taking time to comment on the presentation of this material by which he helped us to give the possible set of readers a better insight into our aims and goals which are clearly understood as the scientists responsibility to inform the decision makers and users about the state of the art and the future perspectives of the products they are using. I therefore hope that his report will be welcomed by the high-tech community around the world.

2   Scope of the Workshop

2.1   The Rôle of Public-Key Cryptography

During the fifteen-year period since its invention the concept of public-key cryptography has completely changed the field of information security.

Secrecy, the classical function of cryptography, has not remained the primary topic of secure systems in the open high-tech community. Instead, the problems of authentication, identification and integrity verifications made clear that the primary topic is rather the notion of **trust**, its generation, transport, preservation and management in complex systems. Owing to modern mathematical research, the invention of the concept of one-way functions has provided an algorithmic tool to develop mechanisms for trust handling.

For reasons still to be discovered the only known public-key algorithms are based on data structures closely related to the areas of Algebra and Computational Number Theory. Results from these areas form the main part of this report, showing that the essential direction for the future development of what is still called **"Public-Key Cryptography"** is rather that of preserving **trust** than that of preserving secrecy, only!

3 List of Topics Chosen Through Self-Assessment

Following the long-standing tradition at the *Mathematisches Forschungsinstitut Oberwolfach* a detailed selection of topics to be covered had not been imposed on or issued to the participants before the meeting.

Alternatively, a list of the most interesting and important topics was discussed by the participants as the first task of the workshop. As the meeting developed more emphasis was placed on certain topics requiring more in-depth consideration based on short self-assessment reviews following each session. The topics initially defined are given in the following list.

- State of the Art in Factoring

- Factoring, Primality Tests and other Applications using Elliptic Curves

- Relations between Computing the Discrete Logarithm and Factoring

- (Fast) Generation of Primes (with certain properties)

- Comparison of the so called RSA-Scheme and Public-Key Cryptosystems based on the Discrete Logarithm

- Other known Public-Key Cryptosystems

- Fast Computation for Public-Key Cryptosystems

- Embedding Public-Key Cryptosystems in Protocols

- Hash Functions and their Interface to Public-Key Cryptosystems

- Specific Hash Functions

- Lifetime and Use of Systems

The topics that finally crystallized through the self-assessment reviews are represented by the structure of the following sections.

4 Short Classification and Description of the Most Prominent Public-Key Systems

Stemming from classical cryptology, which has been almost exclusively based on the use of symmetric encryption functions and the goal of secrecy, the invention of so called public-key systems led to a finer distinction between the different types of crypto functions. While the distinction between symmetric and asymmetric ciphers was the first step, the finer distinction of different types of asymmetric ciphers requires to distinguish between zero-, one-, two- or multi-key systems today.

- One-key systems are symmetric ciphers which essentially do encryption and decryption with the same key, or with two keys either of which is easily derived from the other.

- Two-key ciphers are functions which can serve as primitives for public-key systems since encryption and decryption require different keys or abilities of users.

  Amongst these trapdoor one-way functions constitute the most important class. Usually there are complexity barriers which make it computationally infeasible to derive one key from the knowledge of the other key or of the general system.

- Multi-key systems are based on asymmetric ciphers which are used in protocols for larger systems in applications like access control, shared control, multi-signature schemes etc. with computational barriers between the various keys similar to those in the case of two-key ciphers.

- No-key ciphers are functions which can be applied without a special key and for which inversion is considered an intractable problem. Amongst these are

  - proper one-way functions usually considered as being bijections,

  - hash functions which are in general compressing and therefore not injective.

4.1   One-Way Functions

Proper one-way functions are bijections Φ which allow efficient computation, but for which the inversion Φ^{-1} is considered computationally intractable. They form an important class of primitives in public-key technology today. The most prominent representatives are one-way functions based on NP-complete problems or algebraic equations whose solution is considered computationally intractable. Two instances are the general knapsack problem and problems based on the word problem for algebraic (semi-)groups.

4.1.1   General Knapsacks

General knapsacks have been successfully considered as proper one-way functions for signature purposes [87]. These use a given cargo vector which is multiplied by a general weight distribution and are hard problems for which an inversion seems to be infeasible to find, belonging to the class NPC. However, specially chosen weight distributions allowing the construction of so called trapdoors almost always reduce this problem to a more special one, still being hard, but generally not computationally infeasible (see section 4.2.1).

4.1.2   Discrete Log Problems (Diffie-Hellman, etc.)

While a general theory of one-way functions based on the word problem for algebraic (semi)-groups has been only marginally discussed (c.f. [88, 89]), for the special class of cyclic groups the general word problem reduces to the so called *discrete logarithm problem*. I.e. given an arbitrary element X from a cyclic group G of order $|G|$ generated by a primitive element ω, find the unique integer $x \in [0, |G| - 1]$ with $X = \omega^x$. The difficulty of this problem depends on the representation of the group and its order. If the representation of the group is chosen in too simple a manner, e.g. $G = \left(\mathbb{Z}/n\,\mathbb{Z}, +\right)$, the discrete logarithm problem reduces to simple division, as known from the investigation of linear congruential pseudo-random generators [49].

The Diffie-Hellman exponentiation in a finite group is one of the basic methods to realize the well known commutative key exchange scheme [36]. Usually the multiplicative group of a finite field $GF(p)$ or $GF(2^n)$ is used, while the underlying idea works in any group.

Let G be a finite group, $\omega \in G$. Alice and Bob individually chose secret random integers a and b. Alice sends $A := \omega^a$ to Bob and Bob returns $B := \omega^b$ to Alice (see fig. 1).

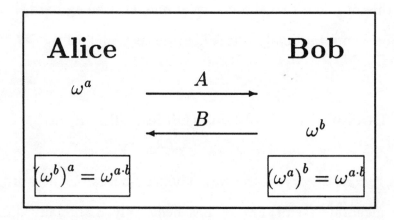

Figure 1: The commutative key-exchange scheme à la Diffie-Hellman, based on exponentiation.

Alice computes: $(B)^a = \left(\omega^b\right)^a = \omega^{a \cdot b}$,

Bob computes: $(A)^b = \omega^{a \cdot b}$, thus both have the same key at hand.

For Alice and Bob it is easy to calculate the common key $\omega^{a \cdot b}$. There is no algorithm known to find $\omega^{a \cdot b}$ from ω, ω^a, ω^b without calculating either the "discrete logarithm" a from ω and ω^a or b from ω and ω^b in the group G. The groups usually used for this system are:

The Multiplicative Group in GF(p): The Original Pohlig-Hellman Scheme

The original Pohlig-Hellman scheme on which the invention of the Diffie-Hellman protocol based uses the multiplicative group G of a Galois Field GF (p) of prime order, in which the problem of taking discrete logarithms was exploited for the first time. The complexity of taking the discrete logarithm is discussed in section 5.2.2.

The Discrete Log Problem in other Finite Fields

The group best suited for implementation is the multiplicative group of a finite field of characteristic 2. Algorithms to find discrete logarithms in GF $(2^n)^*$ are discussed in section 5.2.1.

The Discrete Log Problem in other Algebraic Groups

One of the most important of the remaining groups is that of an elliptic curve over a finite field. The most interesting candidates are elliptic curves over GF (2^n) and GF (p) [12, 50, 73]. Also hyperelliptic curves and special algebras with large groups have been proposed [51].

The Discrete Log Problem in General Groups

The idea to use non-abelian groups, such as $GL(n, q)$, etc., comes up frequently, and is one of the topics that should be investigated in the near future. Little is known about solving the "discrete logarithm problem" in non-abelian groups.

4.2   Trapdoor One-Way Functions

The class of two-key functions as a special class of asymmetric ciphers has largely been used as a synonym for public-key systems according to the following distinction of public-key systems from private-key systems: Two-key systems are essentially one-way systems if considered by outsiders, while insiders can use the inherent trapdoor to invert the bijection Φ in an effective manner.

The basic mathematical idea underlying such constructions is to present the bijection Φ in an algebraic data structure A which enables effective computation of Φ, but makes the inversion Φ^{-1} intractable in the form of its "superficial" presentation. However, the system is designed in such that it can be transformed into an isomorphic data structure TA in which the computation of the inverse mapping $T\Phi^{-1}T^{-1}$ can be carried out in an efficient i.e. easy manner. For the sake of better understanding we call such an isomorphism an *easomorphism*. The two best known algebraic structures for which such *easomorphisms* exist are combinatorial transformations such as easy "superincreasing" knapsacks, graph isomorphism problems etc. or algebraic transformations on well known (commutative) algebras such as the Wedderburn decomposition of semi-simple rings. Special cases are the primary decomposition of vector space endomorphisms as used in

- the analysis of linear recurring sequence generators (see [8, 45]),

- the Fast Fourier Transform [7], which has been used in the design of the newly proposed hash function (see section 4.3),

- the *Chinese Remainder Theorem* as being used in the classical RSA scheme.

The most prominent representatives of these problems are trapdoor knapsacks and the RSA cryptosystem.

4.2.1   Trapdoor Systems Based on Transformed NP-Complete Problems

Trapdoor Knapsacks

The knapsack problem is derived from the idea of packing things (out of a given stock) into a knapsack without leaving space. The simplest case is the one dimensional $\{0,1\}$-knapsack:

For a vector of weights or *cargo vector* [37] $A = (a_1, \ldots, a_n)$ of integers and a binary vector $B \in \{0,1\}^n$, given $S = B \cdot A$ it is hard to find the vector B. On the other hand it is easy to check if the elements of the set $\{b_i\, a_i,\ i = 1, \ldots, n\}$ add up to the given integer: $S = A \cdot B$?

For randomly chosen cargo vectors A this one dimensional knapsack problem is NP-complete. If A is chosen in a special way, the problem of finding the subvector B from the given sum S becomes *simple*. (For example: Let $a_i := 2^{i-1}$ be the components of the cargo vector, then the subvector B to a given sum $S = \sum_{i=1}^{n} b_i\, 2^{i-1}$ is $B := (b_1, \ldots, b_n)$.)

To calculate the subvector B from given cargo vector A and sum S the following idea was proposed by Merkle and Hellman [68]: Start with a simple knapsack problem with cargo vector $A' = (a'_1, \ldots, a'_n)$ and convert it into a more complex one. This can be done by choosing an integer $m > \sum_{i=1}^{n} a_i'$ and an integer w, relatively prime to m. All this information has to be kept secret.

With the public cargo vector $A := (w\, a_1 \bmod m, \ldots, w\, a_n \bmod m)$, the message x is encrypted to $S := x \cdot A$. The message S can be transformed to the integer $S' := w^{-1} S$, using the secrets m and w. The integer S' can be decrypted to the message x by solving the simple knapsack problem $S' = \sum_{i=1}^{n} a_i'\, x_i$.

In 1982 Shamir broke this system [96]. He found a way to reduce the hard knapsack problem to a simple one, not necessarily producing the original w^{-1}, but one that will reveal the original message. To avoid this attack the system was modified to the iterated knapsack, but this system did not live much longer than the original one, see [2, 16].

A more detailed overview of the story of knapsack public-key systems can be found in [17, 32, 37].

The McEliece Cryptosystem

In 1978 McEliece proposed a similar system [65]. This system makes use of the fast decoding algorithm for Goppa codes and the NP-completeness of the decoding problem of general linear codes.

The Goppa code G used for this system is transformed into a "general linear code G'". Therefore the fast decoding algorithm is not applicable any more. A message x is multiplied by the public encoding matrix of the code G' and a random noise vector is added to this product. Decoding this vector to a code word of a general linear code is an NP-complete problem. Transforming the code word to the secret code G and decoding it by the fast decoding algorithm for Goppa codes can be done fast.

While the idea of this system is similar to the one of the knapsack problem, a similar attack is not known. The security of the McEliece cryptosystem is still discussed. Few attacks have been proposed, but none of them seems to endanger the idea of the system [1, 52, 55, 104]. Researchers from Leningrad have recently (Eurocrypt 91) reported a cryptanalytic attack relying on an efficient polynomial time algorithm for decoding linear codes, but the validity of their work is in question and remains to be verified.

4.2.2   Trapdoor Systems Based on the Decomposition of Algebras (RSA, etc.)

The RSA Cryptosystem: The Chinese Remainder Theorem for Two Primes

In 1977, Rivest, Shamir and Adleman proposed a new public-key cryptosystem [82]. It makes use of elementary number theory:

The secret is a pair of two distinct large prime numbers p and q. The public-key is the product $n := pq$ together with an exponent e. The encryption of a message x is taking the e-th power $x^e \bmod n$. If only $x^e \bmod n$, n and e are known, it is hard to recover the message x. If the factorisation $n = pq$ is known, then it is simple to find the e-th root $\bmod n$:

For the Euler function $\varphi(n) = \varphi(p)\,\varphi(q) = (p-1)\,(q-1)$ the following relation holds:

$$x^{k \cdot \varphi(n)+1} \equiv x \quad \bmod n \quad \text{for } k \in x\mathbf{N} \; .$$

Using the known factors p and q it is easy to calculate some $d \in \mathbf{N}$ with[1]: $e \cdot d \equiv 1 \bmod \varphi(n)$. Using this secret key d, x^e can be decrypted to the plaintext:

$$x \equiv \left(x^{\varphi(n)}\right)^k x = x^{k\,\varphi(n)+1} = x^{e\,d} = (x^e)^d \quad \bmod n \; ,$$

where $e \cdot d = k\,\varphi(n) + 1$.

Most attacks on the RSA–system work by factoring the number n. One of the open problems is whether breaking the system is equivalent to the factorisation of n.

---

[1]It is a necessary condition that $\gcd(e, \varphi(n)) = 1$.

J-Algebras

The structure of Wedderburn decomposable algebras, so called J(acobson)-algebras was proposed immediately after the original publication of the RSA system by Simmons [102] on a basis for general asymmetric cryptoschemes. Later it has also been discussed by Beth [7]. Candidates for such algebras were group algebras and polynomial algebras. The basic idea is that since a finite J-ring is necessarily the direct sum of finite fields, the inversion of operations (multiplication, exponentiation etc.) in the ring is equivalent in computational difficulty to finding the ring decomposition, which is equivalent to the factoring of a polynomial into irreducible factors. The idea was quickly abandoned owing to the invention of efficient factorisation algorithms for polynomials (Lenstra [56], etc.). It is however interesting to note, that although these factorisation algorithms are in the class P, the degree of the complexity polynomial is so large, that it may be of some interest to reconsider these structures for possible applications.

Special Polynomial Semi-Groups, Dickson-Polynomials, Rédei-Polynomials etc.

This topic has been intensively studied by several investigators [105, 62, 54], nevertheless for many reasons the results here have not been considered more thoroughly by the general community.

The System of Zheng, Matsumoto and Imai (1989)

In [106] a cryptosystem based on a special type of transformations is suggested. With this type of transformations the authors construct several concrete block ciphers with the following properties.

- Security of the cipher does not depend on any unproven hypothesis.

- Security of the cipher is supported by convincing evidence.

- All design criteria for the cipher are made public.

- The cipher can easily be implemented with current technology.

The security of this system has not been discussed thoroughly yet. The next few years will show if it will be used in practice.

4.3 Hash Functions

A few comments should be made about cryptographic hash functions.[2] Undoubtedly, any reasonable signature scheme has to make use of a

---

[2]The name *hash function* has many synonyms, e.g. *compression function, contraction function, message digest, fingerprint* and *cryptographic checksum*.

hash function because of the following reasons:

- The hash function chains the single blocks of a message to prevent an easy modification of the message by interchanging, introduction or removal of message blocks.

- It destroys possibly existing homomorphic properties of the signature scheme used to prevent attacks which use these properties.

- The computational effort of the signing procedure is much lower because instead of signing every block only a single hash value has to be signed per message.

We give a brief survey on existing hash functions and attacks that have been published:

- The hash function proposed in the ISO/CCITT Document X.509 Annex D was successfully attacked by D. Coppersmith in 1989 [26]. This attack plays an important role in the discussion of properties of a good hash function. It works only if the sender is willing to sign arbitrary messages and if the hash function is used in combination with RSA signatures because it is based on the multiplicative nature of the RSA scheme. It is in question whether the absence of this multiplicative structure is a necessary condition for a good hash function. Maybe we could produce an infinite list of similar other structural properties a hash function must not have.

- An attack on the hash function *N-Hash* [72] that has some similarities to *Feal* [71, 99] was presented at EUROCRYPT '91 by E. Biham and A. Shamir using *Differential Cryptanalysis* [13]. To prevent an easy production of collisions with this attack more than six rounds have to be used in N-Hash. The use of (too) many rounds may contradict the requirement that a hash function should be easily and fast computable.

- G. B. Agnew, R. C. Mullin, I. M. Onyszchuk and S. A. Vanstone proposed a hash function based on iterated exponentiation in $GF(2^{593})$ [6]. In that scheme a message is divided into 593-bit blocks. The blocks are successively exponentiated beginning with the first message block where each exponent depends on the result of the previous computation. The first exponent is given by an initialization vector.

- A hash function called *Snefru* was developed by R. C. Merkle [69] at the Xerox Corporation and published via the Internet. Several weaknesses of this function are already known and a further attack of Snefru was presented by E. Biham and A. Shamir at EUROCRYPT '91 [13] and CRYPTO '91 [14]. The two pass Snefru has been completely cryptanalysed. The four pass Snefru would require $\approx 2^{445}$ evaluations for its cryptanalysis.

- *LOKI*, a 64-bit key/64-bit block cryptosystem similar to DES was presented by L. Brown, J. Pieprzyk and J. Seberry at AUSCRYPT '90. It operates in two modes as a hash function. E. Biham and A. Shamir showed at CRYPTO '91 [14] an easy way to find collisions when LOKI is used as a hash function.

- R. L. Rivest presented the *MD4 Message Digest Algorithm* at CRYPTO '90 [83]. R. C. Merkle [70] has shown that collisions can be found for the first two rounds of MD4. One year later, at CRYPTO '91, B. den Boer and A. Bosselaers showed that a partial attack on the last two rounds of MD4 is possible as well [15].

- An improved version of MD4 called *MD5* was proposed by R. L. Rivest recently [84], it has not yet had much public investigation.

- A new algorithm by C. P. Schnorr [92] that hashes messages of arbitrary length into an 128-bit hash value was presented during the workshop. This algorithm is designed to make the production of a pair of colliding messages computationally infeasible and has some provable properties. A few months later at ASIACRYPT '91 J. Daemen, A. Bosselaers, R. Govaerts and J. Vandewalle presented a program that finds collisions for this hash function within a few hours on a PC [27].

- Its has been shown by M. Naor and M. Yung in [78] and by J. Rompel in [85] how to construct secure one-way hash functions under the assumption that one-way functions ([85]) respectively one-way permutations ([78]) exist. Although this result is rather theoretical it should be mentioned here.

Remarks and Comments

This list shows that the construction of a "good" cryptographic hash function still is an unsolved problem. Several questions have to be answered.

What are the necessary properties of a "good" hash function (collision freeness, etc.)? Many different definitions exist but there is no consensus in sight.

Is it necessary to make assumptions about the distribution of the source of messages to be hashed or can we design a hash function which is suited equally well for natural language and program code?

Should the reduction, removal or introduction of redundancy be an integral part of the hash function — they will be identified as integrity primitives in section 7 — or is it better to regard this as an independent operation which has to be carried out before hashing?

The practical importance of this problem and many more open questions motivated us to propose a follow-up meeting on "Hash Functions". The E.I.S.S. plans to organize a workshop addressing this topic in early 1992.

5 Public-Key Cryptography Depending on Computational Number Theory

The brief classification in section 4 shows, that nearly all public-key systems of practical importance today are based on problems of computational algebra and especially those of computational number theory, since the data structures needed for their application are readily implementable and therefore prime candidates for technical realisations. The essential problem concerning the construction of what we loosely have called easomorphisms is the problem of applying the Chinese remainder transform to composite modular residue rings, which *cum grano salis* is today considered to be the consequence of the

- factorisation problem of integers or

- the word problem for commutative groups which is considered to be the problem of taking discrete logarithms.

Both problems are intrinsically related and closely connected to recent research in computational number theory, the present state of the art of which will be surveyed in the following sections.

5.1   Factorisation of Large Integers

The security of many cryptosystems relies on the assumption that factoring large integers is a computationally infeasible problem. In the following, different methods for factoring integers are discussed from a practical point of view. The most important and most practical algorithms are:

- the elliptic curve method (ECM)

- the double large prime variation of the multiple polynomial quadratic sieve (ppmpqs)

- the number field sieve (NFS).

Beside these methods there are other algorithms which are still of great interest. Especially the Pollard $(p-1)$-method is successful, when $p-1$ is sufficiently smooth. Another approach by C. Schnorr reduces factoring integers and computing discrete logarithms to Diophantine approximation. At the present state of the art, this method is not competitive. But improved lattice reduction algorithms could speed up this type of factoring algorithms ([93, 94]).

In the following the complexity of the algorithms is expressed with the following function:

$$L_n\left[\gamma, \alpha\right] := \exp((\alpha + o(1))(\log n)^{\gamma}(\log \log n)^{1-\gamma}).$$

This function interpolates between the exponential time complexity ($\gamma = 1$) of the trial division algorithm and a polynomial time ($\gamma = 0$) function.

5.1.1   The Elliptic Curve Method

The elliptic curve method (ECM) is an analogue of Pollard's $(p-1)$-method. It was invented by Hendrik Lenstra, Jr. [58].

Attempting to factor an integer N with the elliptic curve method an elliptic curve $E \bmod N$ and a starting point $P \in E$ are selected. Considering the equation:

$$E : y^2 z = x^3 + axz^2 + bz^3 \quad \bmod N$$

for the elliptic curve with $\gcd(4a^3 + 27b^2, N) \neq 1$, a point $P = (x : y : 1)$ can be chosen on the curve. A multiple k is selected, built up from small primes up to a certain bound w.

Small primes should occur several times in k. E.g. $k = \operatorname{lcm}(1, 2, \ldots, w)$ can be chosen for a suitable bound w.

In the next step one calculates the point $k \cdot P \in E(\mathbf{Z}/N\mathbf{Z})$. If $k \cdot P = (x : y : z)$, one calculates $\gcd(z, N)$. The algorithm stops if this gcd is a non-trivial divisor of N. If the method is not successful for a certain k, then one changes the pair (E, P) and starts all over again. This is the basic version of the algorithm.

The method can be practically improved by assuming to have missed the order of the point P on E only by one prime number larger than the bound w (see [75]) in the case the method is not successful. Thus one additionally computes $q \times (kP)$ for some additional primes q. This can be done incrementally in an efficient way. This improvement is due to P. Montgomery and R. Brent.

By applying the ECM, one can expect not to miss factors between 20 and 30 digits. But despite the enormous computational effort during the last few years, up to now, a factor larger than 38 digits has never be found using the ECM. It is estimated that in future by better implementations and using super computers like the Maspar, this upper limit may be increased to up to 40 digits. A speed-up can be achieved by the FFT-extension of the ECM (see [76]). On the other hand it is considered unlikely that the ECM will ever be able to find factors of 50 or more digits.

5.1.2   Double Large Prime Variation of the Multiple Polynomial Quadratic Sieve

At the moment this variation of the quadratic sieve is the fastest practical algorithm for factoring general integers consisting of two large primes.

A common idea of the sieve methods to factor a large integer N is to find a non-trivial congruence of the type

$$x^2 \equiv y^2 \quad \text{mod } N.$$

Then the $\gcd(x + y, N)$ respectively $\gcd(x - y, N)$ is very likely to be a non-trivial factor of N. The congruence is set up in a two-stage algorithm. In the first stage a great number of equations of the type

$$square \equiv B\text{-}smooth \quad \text{mod } N$$

is collected, where *B-smooth* means being built up from prime factors smaller than a bound B.

Out of the exponents of the prime factors on the right hand side a matrix is set up in the second stage. By application of a structured, intelligent Gaussian elimination to this matrix a square can be constructed. In principle one searches for a linear combination of rows in this matrix such that a row with even exponents is found. Once this step is done, one has found a congruence of the type $x^2 \equiv y^2 \text{ mod } N$ and hereby possibly a factor. The quadratic sieve factoring algorithm was originally proposed by Kraitchik. In an improved version due to C. Pomerance the polynomial

$$f(x) = (x + \lfloor \sqrt{N} \rfloor)^2 - N$$

is used to collect the equations. The variable x varies over an interval $[-M, M]$. The value $f(x)$ has to be checked for B-smoothness. This is done by using a sieve on a factor base

$$\left\{ p \mid p < B, p \text{ prime and the Legendre symbol } (N/p) = 1 \right\}.$$

With this method numbers with 50 digits can be factored. A further improvement proposed by P. Montgomery uses multiple polynomials instead of the $f(x)$ above ([101, 22]). Thus the interval for the variable x can be chosen smaller. The average value for the polynomial in x is smaller and consequently the probability of being B-smooth rises.

In particular the general quadratic polynomial

$$Q(x) = ax^2 + bx + c$$

is considered. The parameters a, b and c have to fulfill the integer constraint:

$$b^2 - 4ac = kN$$

in order to assure that we have a square $\mathrm{mod}\, N$. At the same time

$$\sup\left\{|Q(x)| \mid x \in [-M, M]\right\}$$

should be minimized. Thus a good choice for the coefficients is:

$$a \approx \frac{\sqrt{kN}}{M\sqrt{2}}, \quad b \approx 0, \quad c \approx \frac{-M\sqrt{kN}}{\sqrt{8}}.$$

Using this improvement numbers with $70 - 80$ digits can be factored.

Another method to speed up the algorithm is to save not only those x, where $Q(x)$ is B-smooth, but also those with an additional large prime factor. Finding two relations with the same additional large prime, one gets easily a relation within the factor base. This variation is called the large prime variation of the multiple polynomial quadratic sieve (pmpqs). It can be further improved in the following way: allow $Q(x)$ to have two additional factors somewhat larger than B. For every such relation an edge is added to a graph consisting of prime numbers. Every cycle in that graph gives an additional relation with all factors within the factor base. The cross-over point between pmpqs and the later double large prime variation ppmpqs lies in the range of 85 to 90 digit numbers according to practical experience ([61]).

The heuristically expected running time of the algorithm is $L_n [1/2, 1]$. The largest number factored by ppmpqs has 116 decimal digits. This computation took 400 MIPS · years (million instructions per sec. times years = total number of instructions) and was distributed over a world-wide network of workstations, communicating using electronic mail.

Using the run time estimates for ppmpqs, one finds that factoring 512-bit numbers is 1300 times more difficult than factoring 116 digits. Factoring a 512-bit number would thus require about 500.000 MIPS · years, which makes it an exceedingly hard, but not impossible computation for the first stage. The second stage would require approximately 300 Gbyte of storage and 7 months on a $16K$-processor Maspar.

5.1.3   The Number Field Sieve (NFS)

The number field sieve is currently supposed to be the asymptotically fastest known algorithm for factoring integers. It is conjectured to run in time

$$L_n\left[\frac{1}{3}, O(1)\right],$$

but this has not been rigorously proven.

The initial idea of the number field sieve is due to John Pollard (1988), who proposed it for the factorisation of a very special class of numbers; the Cunningham numbers of the form $r^e \pm s$, with r and s small. The modifications necessary to make it applicable to general N are due to Joe Buhler, Carl Pomerance, Hendrik W. Lenstra, Jr. and L. Adleman [59, 3]. Like the several variations of the quadratic sieve algorithms, the number field sieve attempts to factor N by solving the congruence

$$x^2 = y^2 \quad \mathrm{mod}\ N,$$

subject to $x \neq \pm y \mod N$. Namely then $\gcd(x \pm y, N)$ is for each choice of the sign possibly a non-trivial divisor of N.

As explained for the quadratic sieve algorithms one looks for solutions

$$\textit{``square''} \equiv \textit{``smooth''} \ \mathrm{mod}\ N$$

instead of

$$\textit{``square''} \equiv \textit{``square''} \ \mathrm{mod}\ N.$$

Using linear algebra over GF (2), one can multiply many solutions of

$$\text{``square''} \equiv \text{``smooth''}$$

into one solution of "square $\equiv$ square". Also a solution of

$$\text{``smooth''} \equiv \text{``smooth''}$$

can be used (if x and y are smooth with $x = y \bmod N$, then $x^2 = xy \bmod N$ and xy is smooth as well).

The way factoring algorithms often generate smooth numbers is to generate small numbers and exploit the fact that these are more likely to be smooth than large ones. However, in any congruence $x = y \bmod N$ with $x \neq y$ at least one of x, y is larger of equal to $\frac{1}{2}N$ in absolute value, so that x, y cannot both be very small. But this problem can be circumvented by exploiting algebraic number fields.

For a suitable selection of the number field the degree of the number field d is chosen approximately to be

$$d = \left(\frac{3 \log N}{\log \log N} \right)^{\frac{1}{3}}.$$

This means in practice $d \approx 5$ or 6 for integers with 100 to 200 digits. Define $m := \lfloor N^{1/d} \rfloor$ and write N in base m:

$$N = \sum_{i=0}^{d} a_i m^i.$$

This implies $a_d = 1$, $0 \le a_{d-1} \le d$ and all other $a_i < m$. Define a polynomial:

$$f(X) = \sum_{i=0}^{d} a_i X^i \in Z[X].$$

This can be supposed to be irreducible, otherwise a factorisation of n is already found, which is very unlikely to happen.

Let α be a root of the polynomial f. Then the ring $Z[\alpha]$ is considered being a subring of the number field $Q(\alpha)$. The algorithm works in the ring the elements of which can be thought of as vectors:

$$Z[\alpha] = Z \cdot 1 + Z \cdot \alpha + \ldots + Z \cdot \alpha^{d-1}.$$

The addition can be calculated componentwise and the multiplication has to be reduced modulo f.

The following isomorphism is important for the design of the algorithm: The ring $Z[\alpha]$ modulo the ideal $(\alpha - m)$, nothing more than evaluating the polynomials in the ring at m is isomorphic to the integers modulo N:

$$Z[\alpha]/(\alpha - m) \cong Z/NZ.$$

This isomorphism is used to collect equations of the type:

$$\text{``small''} = \text{``small''}$$

in the following way:

$$a + b\alpha = a + bm \mod (\alpha - m).$$

The left hand side takes place in the abstract ring and the right hand side in the integers modulo N.

What is the meaning of "*small*" for the number field? It is determined by the size of the coefficients of the polynomial f and the vector size of the elements considered.

Out of this understanding of "*small*", the smoothness has to be considered, according to the factorisations by ideals in the abstract ring. This ring generally is not a unique factorisation domain, thus the known techniques from the quadratic sieves cannot be applied.

The representation of elements of $Z[\alpha]$ as sequences of exponents indexed by prime ideals is neither injective nor surjective. Especially they are not sufficient for the recognition of squares. But this problem can be solved by the use of quadratic characters ([3]). Thus for the NFS algorithm two different factor bases are needed, one for the abstract ring and one for the integers modulo N.

The number field sieve is not only theoretically a very interesting algorithm. It is remarkably fast in factoring very large integers of a special kind. For integers, that can be represented as a small polynomial with small coefficients, especially such of the form

$$r^e + s, \text{ with } r, s \text{ small},$$

it is substantially faster than ppmpqs. However, these are only a small fraction of the entire set of integers and there is no method known for determining when such a representation is possible.

What can be said about general integers? Based on the analysis of norms that arise in the computation, it can be shown that the crossover point for general integers with the ppmpqs is somewhere between 140 and 150 digits. An implementation and running time analysis on a variety of numbers between 30 and 90 digits has been made. Extrapolation of this data confirms the theoretical crossover estimate. Thus it is not unlikely that the number field sieve is better than the ppmpqs for factoring numbers in the 512-bit range.

5.1.4   Exploiting the Power of Distributed Computing

The three factorisation algorithms mentioned above can be implemented straightforward on parallel computers. A very important point is, that one can distribute a lot of tasks to different processors without the need to receive all answers. Additionally it is very easy to prove the correctness of these processor answers.

This makes these algorithms well suited for distributed computing, allowing to collect idle-times of e.g. workstations not only of participants in a local area network but distributed over a wide network, possibly across the whole world. This was done with the factorisation of the ninth Fermat number and also for the 116 digit number mentioned above, the communication was done by email.

Another possibility is to distribute transaction files to different LAN's, connected by internet. A master daemon requests processing time from local daemons, which are monitoring the LAN participants' idle-times and occasionally use these resources for the tasks requested.

Such systems are partially already in use or are going to be implemented. Using such systems one has to be very careful neither to disturb the integrity nor the sovereignty, nor the comfort of the network participants.

5.2 Discrete Logarithms

Many public key cryptosystems are based on the intractability of discrete logarithms (dlog) calculation in certain cyclic groups. The most important groups for this purpose that initially have been suggested for key exchange systems like the Diffie and Hellman systems are:

- the multiplicative group of finite fields of characteristic 2: $GF(2^n)^*$

- the multiplicative group of prime fields: $GF(p)^*$

- elliptic curve groups over finite fields F: $EC(F)$.

The essential feature seems to be the presentation of the group, even if its structure is to be mathematically trivial. Many more groups have been suggested in different presentations and a large variety of types of groups waits for investigation, like the non-abelian groups with many cyclic subgroups of the same order.

The only discrete logarithm algorithms working in all groups G run in time of around $O(\sqrt{|G|})$. An instance of this algorithm is the Giant-Step-Baby-Step algorithm. It first computes a database of $O(\sqrt{|G|})$ logarithms, requiring a storage amount of that size. Due to the database the calculation of a single logarithm can be reduced to a computation time of $O(\sqrt{|G|})$. This can be done in several ways ([98]).

The cyclic group used for cryptosystems must not have an order containing small prime factors only. Otherwise the discrete logarithm problem can easily be cat into smaller tasks by the Chinese Remainder Theorem.

An open problem is whether a trapdoor is possible in systems based on these groups. It would be interesting to have discrete logarithm based systems with trusted authorities, i. e. only the authority can take discrete logs, while nobody else can. A couple of suggestions for this kind of systems have been made but they don't look really sufficient.

One idea has recently been published by U. Maurer and Y. Yacobi [64]. Choose a modulus $n = p_1 \ldots p_k$, with n being hard to factor n, while it is possible to calculate the discrete logarithms in the $GF(p_i)$ for somebody who knows the factorisation of n. The difficulty lies in the opposite requirements "hard to factor" and "possible to calculate the discrete logarithms".

Another rather surprising idea for a trapdoor is mentioned below in section 5.2.2.

It is an open problem whether the use of cyclic subgroups of the multiplicative groups of finite fields, which can help to speed up the cryptosystem, at the same time leads to faster discrete logarithm algorithms.

5.2.1 The Multiplicative Group of Finite Fields of Characteristic 2

For discrete logarithms in $GF(2^n)$ there exists the Coppersmith variant [24] of the Index-Calculus algorithm. It has a heuristic running time of

$$O(\exp(cn^{\frac{1}{3}}(\ln n)^{\frac{2}{3}})).$$

For every type of field a database has to be computed once, which is the major part of the work. Using this database individual discrete logarithms can be computed rather fast. The database is set up in two stages. First sufficiently many equations have to be collected. Afterwards a sparse linear equation system must be solved. The sieving requires almost no memory, and with care fits into machine registers, so is purely CPU bound, whereas factoring sieving tends to be memory-bandwidth bound. The linear equations are to be solved over a large finite field or direct sum of fields, rather than over $GF(2)$. This tends to make equation solving an even tighter bottleneck than it is for factoring.

With the Coppersmith algorithm discrete logarithms in $GF(2^{127})$ can be calculated quite easily on single workstations. It is conjectured that at present discrete logarithms can be computed in fields of characteristic 2 of orders about 2^{500}.

Actually the computations for $GF(2^{227})$ and $GF(2^{313})$ are completely done, for the field $GF(2^{401})$ the sieving stage is done and even for $GF(2^{503})$ there is 30% of the sieving stage done. These calculations use the Coppersmith algorithm and are executed on an nCube-2 massively parallel computer with 1024 processors ([47]).

For every size of order exist only a few groups of such a type suited for public-key cryptosystems. This is an important fact to be aware of, because the large amount of computation time has to be done only once per group.

5.2.2   The Multiplicative Group of Fields of Prime Order

For the calculation of discrete logarithms in prime fields exist different methods [25, 46, 53]. Among the most important are:

- the linear sieve

- the Gaussian integer scheme

- the number field sieve.

The linear sieve is an algorithm derived from a factorisation algorithm by R. Schroeppel. The Gaussian integer scheme is similar to the number field sieve, but works only with quadratic number fields. The asymptotically fastest known algorithm is the number field sieve with a heuristic running time of

$$O(\exp((c + o(1))(\ln p)^{\frac{1}{3}}(\ln \ln p)^{\frac{2}{3}})).$$

This algorithm has been invented by D. M. Gordon.

As for discrete logarithms in finite fields of characteristic 2, the main amount of computing effort has to be done only once per field $GF(p)$. Afterwards individual logarithms can be calculated rather fast. This is a disadvantage for these type of systems from a security point of view. But in the case of prime fields, there is a large variety of different fields for a certain interval of field sizes.

For a field $GF(p)$ with a prime number with 192 bits, a database of discrete logarithms has been successfully computed. For another field with a prime with 224 bits it is reported to be nearly complete. These computations are done on a cluster of SUN workstations.

Extrapolation of the actual running times suggests that discrete logarithms in $GF(p)$ are slightly harder to compute than factorisation is. The difference is estimated to be around 40 bits, i.e. factoring a number n with k bit length requires about the same computational effort as taking discrete logarithms in prime fields of bit size $k - 40$.

An yet rather conceptual idea for a trapdoor in a cryptosystem based on exponentiation in $GF(p)$ which cannot be discovered by outsiders, is the following: Find a prime p such that

$$p \,\Big|\, \sum_i a_i m^i,$$

with a_i small and some m suited for application of the algorithm using a number field sieve. Thus the calculation of the discrete logarithms is easier, while it is not yet clear whether it is possible to check the existence of such representations for an arbitrary p. This trapdoor is yet not very practical since the number field sieve for discrete logarithms in $GF(p)$ is not yet as efficient as it is in the case of factoring. On the other hand it is important to notice that the trapdoor, in case it works, is hidden or difficult to be recognized.

5.2.3   The Elliptic Curve Group over Finite Fields

Elliptic curves over finite fields have the potential to provide small and low cost public-key systems.

In order to implement the Diffie-Hellman key exchange, the El-Gamal public-key system, and related digital signature schemes one looks for a cyclic group in which computation is easy to carry out but in which the discrete logarithm problem is intractable. We consider the log problem intractable if the so called "square root attacks" are the best methods known to compute logarithms in the group. The group associated with points on an elliptic curve over a finite field have the potential to provide cyclic groups of the desired type and, thus, provide relatively small and low cost public-key systems.

Elliptic curves have been studied for many, many years and there is an enormous literature on the subject. In 1985, M. Koblitz [50] and V. Miller [73] independently proposed them as the bases for a public-key cryptosystem. Since that time much work has been done on both their implementation and their security. We will attempt to highlight the work done in these areas.

It is well known that the square root attacks such as "Giant step — Baby step" [49] "Pollard ρ" [80] "Pollard λ" [80] methods apply to arbitrary cyclic groups and, hence, apply to elliptic curves over finite fields. It is unlikely that the more powerful index calculus attacks (which apply to the cyclic group associated with a finite field) can be used directly to compute logarithms in elliptic curves. So far the most significant result related to the security of elliptic curve cryptosystems is the attack of Menezes, Okamoto and Vanstone [66] henceforth, called the MOV attack.

The MOV attack makes use of the Weil pairing (see [100], pp. 95–99) to establish an efficiently computable isomorphism from a cyclic subgroup of the elliptic curve group to a subgroup of the multiplicative groups of some extension of the finite field on which the curve is defined. To be more precise, suppose E is an Elliptic curve and $E(\text{GF}(q))$ is the set of $\text{GF}(q)$-rational points on E where q is a prime or prime power. Let C be a cyclic subgroup of order n in $E(\text{GF}(q))$ and for simplicity we assume $\gcd(n,q) = 1$. Then the Weil pairing gives an isomorphism from C to the cyclic subgroup of order n contained in $\text{GF}(q^k)$ for some suitable k. Since the index calculus attack applies in a finite field the MOV attack shows that the index calculus methods can be applied to elliptic curve groups but only indirectly. Unless k is less than $\log q$ this method is fully exponential in q and hence less efficient then the square root attacks. For most elliptic curves, k will be large rendering the MOV attack impractical. Furthermore this attack applies only to the small and well understood class of supersingular curves. For the class of non–supersingular curves this attack can be rejected successfully [12]. Further research is necessary for a more detailed consideration of these groups.

In order to be secure from the square root attacks it is generally agreed that the order of the group should be divisible by a prime factor with about forty (40) decimal digits. In terms of elliptic curves, this requirement means that the curve should be defined over a field with at least 2^{130} elements. Curves with these properties are in great abundance.

The most efficient algorithm for computing the order of the group of an elliptic curve over a finite field is the one due to R. Schoof [95]. The algorithm has an asymptotic running time of $O(\log^{5+\epsilon} q)$ bit operations which can be improved to $O(\log^8 q)$ by fast multiplication techniques. Heuristic improvements due to Charlap and Robins [23] have also been obtained but only in the case where q is odd. Of considerable interest is the application of Schoof's algorithm to curves defined over fields in the 130 to 200 bit range. A number of researchers ([20],[67]) are considering this problem and significant and practical results are being obtained. For example, it is possible to compute the order of an arbitrary elliptic curve over GF (2^n) for $n = 155$ in about 50 hours on a Sun Sparc station. This time can be reduced substantially with algorithmic improvements and a finite field coprocessor.

Elliptic curves over the finite field GF (2^n) have considerable interest. The arithmetic processors for the underlying finite field are very easy to construct and have relatively low complexity for n in the range 130 to 200. Recently, a device was constructed [5] to perform field arithmetic in $GF(2^{155})$ and do computations on elliptic curves defined over this field. Using Schoof's algorithm and this chip as a finite field coprocessor, it is anticipated that the order of a curve over the field can be determined in minutes rather than hours. Curves over $GF(2^{155})$ can be found such that the order of the curve contains a prime factor on the order of 48 digits.

In the ElGamal signature scheme and its variants, the signature is a pair of elements (s, r). In both the Schnorr scheme [91] and the new NIST proposal [79], r is about the size of the cyclic group where the signing is being done but s is much larger since to obtain adequate security the cyclic group is embedded in one which is considerably larger. (The subgroup of order q in Z_p^* is typically used). ElGamal signatures and their variants over elliptic curves are attractive since both s and r are about the size of the group in which signing is being done.

6 Public-Key Systems: Mistakes and Problems

A large number of published attacks on public-key cryptosystems do not stem from computational number theory, but rather exploit weaknesses due to protocol failures and wrong system application in a certain environment [77, 63]. Homomorphisms like the multiplicative property of RSA may be irrelevant or even desired for certain applications, whereas they are fatal for others. Therefore attention must be given to the embedding of public-key systems into cryptoprotocols and applications.

6.1 Formal Approach to Design and Analysis

In the traditional way of designing and analysing cryptosystems a need for security leads to the design of a cryptosystem based on heuristics and the experience of the designer. The newly-designed system is exposed to an internal security analysis, which mainly is an attempt to cryptanalyse it. This can be done either by adapting an existing algorithm or by designing a new algorithm to break the system or by improving the upper complexity bounds of a hard problem, on which the system is based. If the cryptosystem passes this security analysis it is used for one or more real applications and thus exposed to further external cryptanalysis.

For a combination of these methods with those of term rewriting under associativity-commutativity laws of symbolic computation [42], we refer to the surprising result of C. Meadows [63].

In design and analysis of cryptosystems formal models and formal proofs are used to ensure a certain security of the system. It is depicted in figure 2.

A real world need for security along with an idea of the system designer lead to a formal model which allows to represent the real world need in the formal world. This step from real to formal world is still based on heuristics and on the experience of the cryptosystem designer. At this stage some formal assumptions (such as computational complexity ones) may be introduced, either explicitly or implicitly. It must be shown that these assumptions are reasonable.

The design of the cryptosystem using this approach is equivalent to the formulation of a conjecture in the model, which has to be proven formally. A proof of the negation of the conjecture or the inability to find a proof enforces redesign of the system.

As result of the formal proof the conjecture becomes a theorem. In other words the security of the newly designed cryptosystem is now proven *with respect to the underlying formal model.*

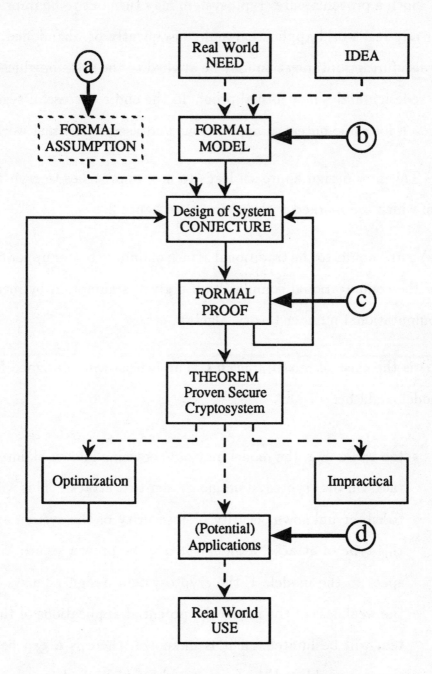

Figure 2: Formal approach to cryptosystem design

Such a proven secure cryptosystem may turn out to be impractical for any real world application and consequently be abandoned. Otherwise further optimization may be applied to the system, which leads to redesign and a new formal proof. In the end a successful system is chosen for some potential applications and used in the real world.

This new design approach leads to new approaches to cryptanalysis, which are marked with (a) to (d) in figure 2.

(a) corresponds to the traditional attack of finding better upper bounds for the computational complexity of a given assumption by means of computational number theory, algebra, etc.

(b) is the class of *model problems*. The heuristically designed formal model could be:

- too weak: E.g. the model may only envision known-plaintext attacks on the cryptosystem, no chosen-text attacks. This will lead to either unknown security or insecurity of the system against this type of attacks, although it may be proven secure with respect to the model. If the cryptosystem designer knows about the weakness of the model the potential applications of the system will be limited. If it is unknown, there is a gap between the real world and the formal world, which can be exploited by an attacker. Note, however, that a too weak model does not necessarily imply a too weak system, since the security of the cryptosystem might still be provable under a stronger model.

- wrong: E.g. the (Feige-)Fiat-Shamir identification scheme [40, 41] can be attacked using the so-called mafia fraud [33], because the model of zero-knowledge interactive proofs is inadequate for identification of individuals in the real world. Note, however, that no satisfactory formal model for identification has been given yet.

- absent: In order to prove "general" results there may be a temptation to use no model at all. However without an underlying model no mathematical proof is possible. It may be possible to find a certain model (corresponding to a certain real world scenario), for which the "general" proof does not hold. (see e.g. [35])

(c) is the possibility that the formal proof is incorrect. This may or may not induce a security weakness. There is e.g. a slight error in the proof of the Fiat-Shamir scheme [41], which leads to an efficient attack [21, 48]. This attack, however, can in turn be avoided by a minor modification of the system, which makes the proof correct.

(d) refers to the application of a proven secure cryptosystem for a case which is not covered by the model in which the security was proven. Again this can (but needs not) introduce successful attacks on the cryptosystem, when used in that particular application. Note that for a published cryptosystem the step of deciding whether the formal model used to design the system is appropriate for a certain real world application, often is no longer in the designer's responsibility. An example of a wrong application is the use of undeniable signatures for software protection [34].

In view of these different potential points of attack it is conceivable that there often will be another way of attacking a system than by means of computational number theory. The formal approach to cryptosystem design, yielding "proven secure" schemes, merely shifts the heuristics from the design of the cryptosystem to the design of the formal model and the check of potential applications against this model.

6.2   Flow of Trust

An important viewpoint for the analysis of a cryptosystem is the flow of trust in the system. Trust in a cryptosystem cannot be created, but only transferred from an initially trusted entity to others. Important questions for the analysis of the trust transfer are:

- Who trusts whom?

- When?

- For what purpose?

For an example two persons (sender and receiver) using a symmetric cryptosystem need to trust each other unconditionally, since the sender can disavow messages that he did send and the receiver can attribute messages to the sender which he did not send. None of these frauds could be proven to an arbiter.

When a key distribution center is introduced it is possible to derive the above mentioned unconditional trust between sender and receiver from an initial unconditional trust between each of them and the key distribution center.

The introduction of a public-key system reduces the unconditional nature of the necessary trust. Sender and receiver need only trust the key distribution center to give them the correct public key of their partner. The sender can no longer disavow messages, nor can the receiver fraudulently attribute messages to him. There is, however, no way to prevent either sender or receiver from revealing his own secret key.

7 Projection of Needs and Requirements for Public-Key Systems

Looking back, the last few years research in Public-Key Cryptography was dominated by the question

What can be done?

and even today this is the "engine" for the majority of new developments in that field. Actually, a much more important question is

What has to be done?

This question has been merely neglected in the past, but dealing with information integrity a great number of functions are needed to satisfy certain requirements. Finding a solution to these tasks might be a better guideline to lead the cryptographer into the future.

Proceeding towards an answer to the second question above we try to identify some *basic requirements*. There are *secrecy* and *authenticity*. The second one can be subdivided into *authenticity* in a stronger sense and *integrity*. The following example motivates distinguishing between these kinds of authenticity.

Consider a communication between two participants over a network. While establishing the communication link the participants want to make sure that they are speaking with the partner they expect. In this the *authenticity* of the participants has to be guaranteed during the session. During the communication the participants want to ensure that the exchanged messages have not been modified during transmission. Now the *integrity* of the messages has to be guaranteed during and after proceeding.

At this point we have a very coarse division into three main requirements. As a second step we try to give a (partial) list of common *information integrity functions*, which result from further subdividing and specialising the three basic requirements:

- Identification

- Authorization

- License and/or Certification

- Signature

- Witnessing (Notarization)

  - blind

  - syntactic

  - semantic

- Concurrence (Agreement)

- Timeliness

- Liability

- Receipts

- Certification of Origination and/or Receipt

- Endorsement

- Access (Egress)

- Validation

- Time of Occurrence

- Authenticity — Files, Software, Processes

- Vote

- Ownership

- Registration

- Approval/Disapproval

- Privacy (Secrecy)

- Money

The distinction between *blind*, *syntactic* and *semantic* notarization must be explained. In the first case a person acts as a witness that some action has taken place — usually the signing of a document — without any knowledge about the contents of the document or the consequences of this action. In the second case the witness is allowed to read the document *without understanding* it. It is obvious, that no human being can read something without understanding it if we assume that it wasn't written in a foreign language. A program can do this task very well. To detect every slight modification of the document it isn't necessary to understand it's meaning. The last case is the most popular in real life and it might be a task for future research to enable programs to *understand* the meaning of documents and to act as witnesses using this knowledge.

Another remark, concerning the authenticity of processes: we observe that distributed computing will becomes increasingly attractive. The growing of LAN's, MAN's and WAN's with higher throughput and an increasing potential of powerful workstations all over the world is one reason for this development. Another reason is that our understanding of parallelism becomes better and better. If a process can change the machine during its execution it is reasonable to speak about the authenticity not only of the software but also of the "living" process because it might become infected by some virus, worm or trojan horse during its change from one processor to another.

For most of this functions several solutions have already been found. Future research will show if it is possible to find solutions for all of them. A possible approach to do this is to identify a set of *information integrity primitives*. The primitives can be regarded as a modular construction system that can be used to build up "higher" integrity functions. The following list gives an example of such a set:

- Secrecy

- Authentication

- Shared Control

- Compression

  - Information Preserving

  - Hashing

- Redundancy

  - Introduction

  - Removal

  - (Truncation)

- "Hiding" Homomorphisms

- Random Number Generation

• Key Distribution

The attentive reader might have observed that e.g. secrecy appears as a basic requirement and as a primitive. It is very difficult to make a *sharp* distinction between requirements, primitives and information integrity functions, this depends always on the individual point of view.[3] But it is not necessary in this context to find a definite classification because we only want to give some kind of *checklist* for the designer of public-key cryptosystems. Therefore we rather quote a point twice than overlook it.

7.1   Assessment and Prediction: Guide Public-Key Systems Implementations in the 1990s

We would like to discuss some limits which have to be considered by the designer of a new cryptographic system which is a realisation of an information integrity function to guarantee within limits that such a system will be resistant against possible cryptanalytic attacks in the future.

If we distinguish between the requirements of secrecy and authenticity it seems to be the easier problem to fulfill the second requirement

---

[3]We have made the experience that at this point usually start endless discussions.

over a long period because in most circumstances there is no use in forging a 50-year old document. So we shall focus on secrecy. Furthermore we observe that information appears in tactical and strategic applications. Information of the second kind may have a much longer lifetime than information of the first kind.

To give an estimate of the average traffic lifetime let's look at table 1. An average traffic lifetime of 50 years seems to be a reasonable estimate.

Type of Traffic	Lifetime
Product Announcements, Mergers, Interest Rates	days or weeks
Trade Secrets (e.g. Coca Cola receipt)	decades
H-bomb Secret	> 40 years
Diplomatic Embarrassments	> 65 years
Identities of Spies	> 50 years
Personal Affairs	> 50 years
U.S. Census Data	100 years

Table 1: Traffic Lifetimes

Table 2 shows the lifetimes of a few cryptosystems being relevant for practical use. Keeping this table in mind, we can assume that a new cryptosystem will be in use for 30 or more years. Storage security systems may be in use much longer.

Cipher	From	To
Enigma	1920's	$\geq$ 1940's
M-209	1930's	$\geq$ today
KL-7	$\approx$1950	$\approx$1980
KW-7	$\approx$1960	$\approx$1990
DES	1975	$\geq$1993

Table 2: Lifetimes of classical Cryptosystems

How will the capabilities of a cryptanalyst change in the future? As expected, computers became faster and memories became bigger and cheaper during the last years but there were also unexpected developments, e.g. the progress in massively distributed computing. Nevertheless a prediction of the hardware developments and the increase of computational power is the minor problem. If we plot the increase of computational power over the years we obtain a rather *smooth* function: approximately, the efficiency of computing equipment divided by price increases by a factor of 10 every 5 years . Thus, in 50 years the aggregate computing power worldwide will be $10^{10+\epsilon}$ times[4] bigger than today! Possibly, there will exist machines in the future who are able to produce other (special purpose) machines whith only one task: breaking cryptosystems.

---

[4]$\epsilon > 0$ expresses a safety margin of some magnitude.

The more serious problem is to give an estimate of the algorithmic developments over the next years. Some improvements could be expected, e.g. better techniques for memory management, but if we compare the plot of the algorithmic power with the plot of the computational power it looks more like a step function than like a smooth function. A few of the most important "steps" in the past were the development of *FFT-Algorithms*, the *Quadratic Sieve*, the *Number Field Sieve* and the Coppersmith attack on discrete logarithms in $GF(2^n)$.

At this point we are able to formulate the challenge for a designer of a new cryptosystem: If the designer starts in 1992 and we assume that the first field use of the new system will be in 2000, it still may be in use in 2030 and encrypt something that must be secret until 2080. At this time the potential of a cryptanalyst results from combining the increase of computational and algorithmic power. Furthermore it can be expected that there will be much more traffic to be intercepted than today.

If we take these factors into account we see that it is extremely difficult to give any exact predictions and guidelines for the future.

If for example someone wants to fix the modulus size of a public-key cryptosystem using modular exponentiation he has to be very careful. It seems to be a better choice to keep the modulus size variable so that it is possible to increase it — if necessary — without discarding the hardware or software and the need to buy new equipment in a progressing manner.

This leads to an interesting problem which should be remarked here. A modification of the modulus size for encryption does not cause the main problem. But, what about digital signatures? If the modulus changes a signature produced with a shorter modulus may become void. The requirement of *long time authenticity* makes it necessary to update the signature. This demand for *re-signing* may lead to new types of attacks similar to the attacks discussed in [28, 30, 31]. It would be an interesting task to develop an *adaptive signature scheme* offering elegant mechanisms for re-signing.

On the other hand we wish to mention that the increasing computational power will also have positive effects. Higher encryption speeds might enable encryption devices handling numbers that are several times longer than the numbers used in today's applications with the same processing time, resulting in a higher level of security. Maybe these improvements will dominate the improvements of the cryptanalyst. Under the assumption that the problems of factorisation and computing discrete logarithms don't collapse totally to a polynomial complexity it might be that in the long run the cryptographer will win the race against the cryptanalyst.

7.2   Some Remarks Concerning Exponentiation Schemes

In this section we would like to discuss some requirements for exponentiation chips for RSA and ElGamal-like systems and the safe use of the RSA scheme in general.[5]

Encryption Speed

There is the old but attractive idea of a worldwide network with a lot of RSA-encrypted messages travelling around. In this concept every participant tries to decrypt every received message by taking the e-th root mod$n$ on the ciphertext.[6] The RSA scheme guarantees that only one receiver is able to read the plaintext. In other words taking the e-th root works like a "filter". This concept is realistic only if computation is fast. If we want to avoid creating a new bottleneck it would be necessary to encrypt and decrypt tens of MBytes of data per second looking on today's traffic speed and volume. After nearly 15 years of research however a short look at table 3 and table 4 shows that we should not be too optimistic that this idea will become feasible

---

[5]Most of what is mentioned in this section applies for other public-key systems using modular arithmetic as well.

[6]In fact he computes the d-th power mod$n$ of the ciphertext where d is his private exponent and n his modulus.

in the near future.[7]

Nevertheless, two interesting alternatives to full-custom RSA-chips should be briefly mentioned here. One important approach to fast exponentiation is to use standard digital signal processors. RSA Data Security presented a system based on the Motorola 56000 DSP. At a clock rate of 30 MHz the system performs a 512-bit exponentiation in 26 ms using 780,000 clock cycles. This leads to a baud rate of 19,692 bps.

Today it is possible to achieve much higher throughput rates if expensive special purpose hardware is used. M. Shand, P. Bertin and J. Vuillemin presented a solution based on *Programmable Active Memories* capable to perform 512-bit exponentiations with 225 Kbits/sec using Chinese remaindering [97].

Further Conclusions

We see that the realistic applications for the RSA scheme (today) are key management and digital signatures. Usually the data itself is encrypted with a common symmetric cryptosystem, e.g. DES. For this reason it does not make sense to argue with high throughput rates of

---

[7]It is not the intention of the table to give a *complete* overview on all existing RSA chips.

Product	Clock Speed	Baud Rate Per 512 Bits	Clock Cycles Per 512 Bit Encryption
Alpha Techn.	25 MHz	13 K	.98 M
AT&T	15 MHz	19 K	.4 M
British Telecom	10 MHz	5.1 K	1 M
Business Sim. Ltd.	5 MHz	3.8 K	.67 M
Calmos Syst. Inc.	20 MHz	28 K	.36 M
CNET	25 MHz	5.3 K	2.3 M
Cryptech	14 MHz	17 K	.4 M
Cylink	16 MHz	6.8 K	1.2 M
Pijnenburg	25 MHz	50 K	.256 M
Plessy Crypto.	—	10.2 K	—
Sandia	8 MHz	10 K	.4 M

Table 3: Existing RSA Chips

Product	Technology	Bits Per Chip	No. of Trans.	Uses CRT Yes/No
Alpha Techn.	2	1024	180,000	—
AT&T	1.5	298	100,000	no
British Telecom	2.5	256	—	—
Business Sim. Ltd.	Gate Array	32	—	—
Calmos Syst. Inc.	2	593	95,000	no
CNET	1	1024	100,000	—
Cryptech	Gate Array	120	33,000	no
Cylink	1.5	1024	150,000	no
Pijnenburg	1.0	1024	400,000	no
Plessy Crypto.	—	512	—	—
Sandia	2	272	86,000	no

Table 4: Existing RSA Chips (continued)

the RSA chips. A more interesting parameter is the time needed to carry out *one single* encryption or decryption including the loading of the keys into the cryptographic device.

Three parameters of a RSA chip play an important rôle and have to be considered if we want to use RSA as an authentication scheme:[8]

- Size of the Modulus

- Speed

- Cost

They depend on the specific application the chip is built for and on the required level of security.

It is not possible to build a general purpose RSA chip which is suited for every application! Table 5 gives some examples for performance requirements depending on different applications. Clearly if the channel which is used in an application has a low bandwidth (say 2500 bps) in most cases the channel dominates the speed of the application and one does not have to worry about the exponentiation speed. In other applications (e.g. ISDN[9] with 64 kbps or more) the exponentiation speed would be the dominating factor. For some

---

[8]It should be obvious that the three parameters depend on each other as well.

[9]ISDN stands for Integrated Services Digital Network.

applications in the military field a high level of security (resulting in a very long modulus) as well as high speed is required. But these special purpose solutions do not have to be cheap. On the other hand a chip which should be available for everybody's PC **has** to be cheap but (in most cases) the required level of security is modest, according to the usage.

Application	Time (seconds)	No. Exp./Side
Login Protocol	1–15	2–5
Secure Telephone Setup	1–15	2–5
TCP 3-handshake	.001–1	2–5
Open a Door	1–5	1
Identification: Friend or Foe	.005	1-5

Table 5: Performance Requirements for Exponentiation Algorithms

Design Criteria

1. Care has to be taken if a RSA chip uses the Chinese remainder technique for speed improvement. Obviously this chip will roughly be up to four times faster than a comparable product but it might be more difficult to hide the factorisation of the modulus (e.g. tempest).[10]

---

[10]The importance of this point has to be relativized due to the fact that the factorisation of the modulus can also be obtained with little computational effort

2. When designing a new chip it would be a good idea to use an architecture based on one *generalized long string shift and add register* which can be adapted to different data structures.

3. A chip designed in that way would be capable for use in both RSA schemes and ElGamal-like schemes as the general computational feature to be provided is exponentiation. Nevertheless for high performance reasons the approach of a dedicated architecture could be chosen [10, 81, 86].

4. It seems to be advisable to make such an exponentiation chip internally partitionable and/or cascadable. That would allow to do modular exponentiations with different modulus lengths, e.g. 512, 768, 896 and 1024 bit each. As mentioned before, public-key cryptosystems based on the discrete logarithm achieve the same amount of security with a smaller modulus size as a comparable RSA system. This fact could be exploited by such a *flexible* architecture. Furthermore that architecture would enable the user to keep pace with the progress in cryptanalysis at maximum use of performance.

5. In many public-key schemes powers of a *fixed* element have to be computed. If one does not use the standard "square-and-multiply" method of exponentiation significant speed improvement can be achieved for the cost of more storage. To perform a

---

if one knows the private key.

512-bit exponentiation using the square-and-multiply scheme on average 767 modular multiplications are needed, using storage of at least 128 bytes. The scheme presented in [18] requires only 104 modular multiplications on the average for the same task, using storage of 23040 bytes. This implies more than a seven-fold speedup on average. The main idea behind this technique is to select a suitable representation of the exponent in a base different from 2 and to precompute a carefully selected set of values that can be used to compute arbitrary powers.

6. Some manufacturers of RSA hardware compare the difficulty of breaking the RSA scheme by factoring the modulus with breaking the DES by an exhaustive key search. This argumentation is often used to stress the amount of "security" the chip provides. We give a warning because these comparisons are ill-defined. First of all for an exhaustive key search a corresponding plain-text/ciphertext pair is needed. To factorize a RSA modulus we only have to know the modulus. Secondly if we want to use special purpose hardware for the two attacks and we are given a fixed amount of money to do that task we need to buy a lot of DES chips on one side. On the other side we do not need additional hardware — the factorisation would be done by a lot of workstations which are already there and which can be used for many other (probably more useful) things.

7. For the most applications a modulus size of 1024 bit for RSA should achieve a sufficient level of security for "tactical" secrets for the next ten years. This is for long-term secrecy purposes, for short-term authenticity purposes 512 Bit might suffice in this century.

Please note: Although the participants of the workshop feel best qualified in their respective areas, this statement (with respect to long lasting security) should be taken with caution.

References

[1] C. M. Adams, H. Meijer; *Security-Related Comments Regarding McEliece's Public-Key Cryptosystem*; Advances in Cryptology — Proceedings of CRYPTO '87, Springer LNCS 293, Berlin 1989, pp. 224–228.

[2] L. M. Adleman; *On Breaking the Iterated Merkle-Hellman Public Key Cryptosystem*; Advances in Cryptology — Proceedings of CRYPTO '82, pp. 303–308.

[3] L. M. Adleman; *Factoring Numbers Using Singular Integers*; Proc. 23nd Ann. ACM Symp. on Theory of Comp. (STOC), 1991, pp. 64–71.

[4] L. M. Adleman, C. Pomerance, R. S. Rumely; *On distinguishing prime numbers from composite numbers*; Ann. of Math. 117, 1983, pp. 173–206.

[5] G. B. Agnew, R. C. Mullin, S. A. Vanstone; *An arithmetic processor for* GF (2^{155}); (in preparation).

[6] G. B. Agnew, R. C. Mullin, I. M. Onyszchuk, S. A. Vanstone; *An Implementation for a Fast Public-Key Cryptosystem*; Journal of Cryptology, v. 3, n. 2, 1991, pp. 63–79.

[7] T. Beth; *Verfahren der schnellen Fourier-Transformation*; Teubner, Stuttgart, 1984.

[8] T. Beth, F. C. Piper; *The Stop-And-Go Generator*; Advances in Cryptology — Proceedings of EUROCRYPT '84, Springer LNCS 209, 1984, pp. 88–92.

[9] T. Beth; *Efficient Zero-Knowledge Identification Scheme for Smart Cards*; Advances in Cryptology — Proceedings of EUROCRYPT '88, Springer LNCS 330, Berlin 1988, pp. 77–95.

[10] T. Beth, D. Gollmann; *Algorithm Engineering for Public Key Algorithms*; IEEE Journal on Selected Areas in Communications, v. 7, n. 4, 1989, pp. 458–466.

[11] T. Beth, S. A. Vanstone, G. B. Agnew; *What One Should Know about Public Key Algorithms — Today !*; SECURICOM '90, 1990, pp. 47–63.

[12] T. Beth, F. Schaefer; *Non Supersingular Elliptic Curves for Public Key Cryptosystems*; Abstracts of EUROCRYPT '91, 1991, pp. 155–159.

[13] E. Biham, A. Shamir; *Differential Cryptanalysis of Feal and N-Hash*; Abstracts of EUROCRYPT '91, 1991, pp. 1–8.

[14] E. Biham, A. Shamir; *Differential Cryptanalysis of Snefru, Khafre, REDOC-II, LOKI and Lucifer*; Abstracts of CRYPTO '91, 1991, pp. 4-1–4-7.

[15] B. den Boer, A. Bosselaers; *An Attack on the Last Two Rounds of MD4*; Abstracts of CRYPTO '91, 1991, pp. 4-19–4-23.

[16] E. F. Brickell; *Breaking iterated knapsacks*; Advances in Cryptology — Proceedings of CRYPTO '84, Springer LNCS 196, 1984, pp. 342–358.

[17] E. Brickell, A. M. Odlyzko; *Cryptanalysis: A survey of recent results*; Proceedings of the IEEE, v. 76, n. 5, 1988, pp. 578–593.

[18] E. F. Brickell, M. Gordon, K. S. McCurley; *Fast Exponentiation with Precomputation*; Presented at Rump session of CRYPTO '91, 1991.

[19] L. Brown, J. Pieprzyk, J. Seberry: *LOKI — A Cryptographic Primitive for Authentication and Secrecy Applications*; Advances in Cryptology — Proceedings of AUSCRYPT '90, Springer LNCS 453, 1990, pp. 229–236.

[20] J. Buchmann, V. Müller; *Computing the number of points of elliptic curves over finite fields*; Proc. of the Int. Symp. on Symbolic and Algebraic Comp. (ISSAC '91), 1991, pp. 179–182.

[21] M. Burmester, Y. Desmedt; *Remarks on Soundness of Proofs*; Electronics Letters 25, 1989, pp. 1509–1510.

[22] T. Caron, R. D. Silverman; *Parallel Implementation of the Quadratic Sieve*; J. Supercomputing, v. 1, n. 3, 1988, pp. 273–290.

[23] L. Charlap, R. Coley, P. Robbins; *Enumeration of rational points on elliptic curves over finite fields*; (preprint).

[24] D. Coppersmith; *Fast evaluation of logarithms in fields of characteristic two*; IEEE Trans. Inform. Theory, IT-30, 1984, pp. 587–594.

[25] D. Coppersmith, A. M. Odlyzko, R. Schroeppel; *Discrete Logarithms in GF(p)*; Algorithmica, v. 1, 1986, pp. 1–15.

[26] D. Coppersmith; *Analysis of ISO/CCITT Document X.509 Annex D*; ISO/IEC JTC1/SC27/ WG20.2 Paper N160, 1989.

[27] J. Daemen, A. Bosselaers, R. Govaerts, J. Vandewalle; *Collisions for Schnorr's Hash Function FFT-Hash Presented at Crypto '91*; Presented at Rump session of ASIACRYPT '91, 1991.

[28] G. I. Davida; *Chosen Signature Cryptanalysis of the RSA (MIT) Public Key Cryptosystem*; Tech. Rept. TR-CS-82-2, Dept. of Electrical Engineering and Computer Science, Univ. of Wisconsin, Milwaukee, 1982.

[29] D. W. Davies, W. L. Price; *Security for Computer Networks — An Introduction to Data Security in Teleprocessing and Electronic Funds Transfer*; John Wiley & Sons, 1984.

[30] D. E. Denning; *Digital Signatures with RSA and Other Public-Key Cryptosystems*; CACM, v. 27, n. 4, 1984, pp. 388–392.

[31] Y. Desmedt, A. M. Odlyzko; *A chosen text attack on the RSA cryptosystem and some discrete logarithm schemes*; Advances in Cryptology — Proceedings of CRYPTO '85, Springer LNCS 218, 1986, pp. 516–522.

[32] Y. Desmedt; *What happened with Knapsack Cryptographic Schemes*; in Performance Limits in Communication, Theory and Practice, NATO ASI Series E: Applied Sciences — Vol. 142, ed. J. K. Skwirzynski, Kluwer Academic Publishers, 1988, pp. 113–134.

[33] Y. Desmedt, C. Goutier, S. Bengio; *Special Uses and Abuses of the Fiat-Shamir Passport Protocol*; Advances in Cryptology — Proceedings of CRYPTO '87, Springer LNCS 293, Berlin 1988, pp. 21–39.

[34] Y. Desmedt, M. Yung; *Weaknesses of Undeniable Signature Schemes*; Abstracts of EUROCRYPT '91, 1991, pp. 111-116.

[35] Y. Desmedt; *A cryptanalytic study of cascade ciphers*; Dept. of EE & CS, Univ. of Wisconsin-Milwaukee, Tech. Report TR–91–6–01, 1991.

[36] W. Diffie, M. Hellman; *New Directions in Cryptography*; IEEE Trans. Inform. Theory, IT-22, n. 6, 1976, pp. 644–654.

[37] W. Diffie; *The First Ten Years of Public-Key Cryptography*; Proceedings of the IEEE, v. 76, n. 5, 1988, pp. 560–576.

[38] T. ElGamal; *A Public Key Cryptosystem and a Signature Scheme Based on Discrete Logarithms*; IEEE Trans. Inform. Theory, IT-31, n. 4, 1985, pp. 469–472.

[39] T. ElGamal; *A subexponential-time Algorithm for Computing Discrete Logarithms over $GF(p^2)$*; IEEE Trans. Inform. Theory, IT-31, 1985, pp. 473–481.

[40] U. Feige, A. Fiat, A. Shamir; *Zero-Knowledge Proofs of Identity*; Journal of Cryptology 1, 1988, pp. 77–94.

[41] A. Fiat, A. Shamir; *How to Prove Yourself: Practical Solutions to Identification and Signature Problems*; Advances in Cryptology — Proceedings of CRYPTO '86, Springer LNCS 263, 1987, pp. 186–194.

[42] A. Fortenbacher; *Effizientes Rechnen in AC-Gleichungstheorien*; Dissertation, Universität Karlsruhe, 1989.

[43] M. R. GAREY, D. S. JOHNSON; *Computers and Intractability. A Guide to the Theory of NP-Completeness.*; Freeman, San Francisco, 1979.

[44] S. Goldwasser, J. Kilian; *Almost all primes can be quickly certified*; Proc. 18th Annual ACM Symp. on the Theory of Computing (STOC), 1986, pp. 316–329.

[45] D. Gollmann; *Pseudo random properties of cascade connections of clock controlled shift registers*; Advances in Cryptology — Proceedings of EUROCRYPT '84, Springer LNCS 209, 1984, pp. 93–98.

[46] D. M. Gordon; *Discrete Logarithms Using the Number Field Sieve*; Preprint, March 28, 1991.

[47] D. M. Gordon, K. S. McCurley; *Computation of Discrete Logarithms in Fields of Characteristic Two (Preliminary Report)*; Presented at Rump session of CRYPTO '91, 1991.

[48] H.-J. Knobloch; *A Smart Card Implementation of the Fiat-Shamir Identification Scheme*; Advances in Cryptology — Proceedings of EUROCRYPT '88, Springer LNCS 330, 1988, pp. 87–95.

[49] D. E. Knuth; *The art of computer programming, Vol. 2: Seminumerical algorithms*, second edition, Addison-Wesley, Reading, MA, 1981.

[50] N. Koblitz; *Elliptic Curve Cryptosystems*; Math. Comp., v. 48, n. 177, 1987, pp. 203–209.

[51] N. Koblitz; *Hyperelliptic Cryptosystems*; Journal of Cryptology, n. 1, 1989, pp. 139–150.

[52] V. I. Korzhik, A. I. Turkin; *Cryptoanalysis of McEliece's Public-Key Cryptosystem*; Abstracts of EUROCRYPT '91, 1991, pp. 27–28.

[53] B. A. LaMacchia, A. M. Odlyzko; *Computation of discrete logarithms in prime fields*; Codes, Designs and Cryptography 1, 1991, pp. 46–62.

[54] H. Lausch, W. Müller, W. Nöbauer; *Über die Struktur einer durch Dicksonpolynome dargestellten Permutationsgruppe des Restklassenringes modulo n*; J. Reine Angew. Math. v. 261, 1973, pp. 88–99.

[55] P. J. Lee, E. F. Brickell; *An Observation on the Security of McEliece's Public-Key Cryptosystem*; Advances in Cryptology — Proceedings of EUROCRYPT '88, Springer LNCS 330, Berlin, 1988, pp. 275–280.

[56] A. K. Lenstra, H. W. Lenstra, Jr., L. Lovácz; *Factoring Polynomials with Rational Coefficients*; Mathematische Annalen, v. 261, n. 4, 1982, pp. 515–534.

[57] H. W. Lenstra, Jr.; *Elliptic curves and number-theoretic algorithms*; Report 86-19, Mathematisch Instituut, Universiteit van Amsterdam, 1986.

[58] H. W. Lenstra, Jr.; *Factoring Integers with Elliptic Curves*; Ann. of Math., v. 126, 1987, pp. 649–673.

[59] A. K. Lenstra, H. W. Lenstra, Jr., M. S. Manasse, J. M. Pollard; *The number field sieve*; Proc. 22nd Ann. ACM Symp. on Theory of Comp. (STOC), Baltimore, 1990, pp. 564–572.

[60] A. K. Lenstra, M. S. Manasse; *Factoring by electronic mail*; Advances in Cryptology — Proceedings of EUROCRYPT '89, Springer LNCS 434, 1990, pp. 355–371.

[61] A. K. Lenstra, M. S. Manasse; *Factoring by electronic mail*; Advances in Cryptology — Proceedings of EUROCRYPT '90, Springer LNCS 473, 1991, pp. 72–82.

[62] Da-Xing Li; *Cryptoanalysis of Public-Key Distribution Systems Based on Dickson Polynomials*; Electronics Letters, v. 27, n. 3, 1991, pp. 228–229.

[63] Mathematisches Forschungsinstitut Oberwolfach; *Mathematical Concepts of Dependable Systems*; Tagungsbericht 17/1990.

[64] U. M. Maurer, Y. Yacobi; *Non-interactive Public Key Cryptography*; Abstracts of EUROCRYPT '91, 1991, pp. 242–247.

[65] R. J. McEliece; *A Public-Key cryptosystem based on algebraic Coding theory*; Deep Space Network Progress Report, Pasadena, Jet Propulsion Labs, 1978, pp. 42–44.

[66] A. Menezes, T. Okamoto, S. A. Vanstone; *Reducing Elliptic Curve Logarithms to Logarithms in a Finite Field*; Proc. of the 22nd Annual ACM Symposium on the Theory of Comp., 1991, pp. 80–89.

[67] A. Menezes, S. A. Vanstone, R. Zucrharato; *Counting points on elliptic curves over F_{2^m}*; (preprint).

[68] R. C. Merkle, M. E. Hellman; *Hiding information and signatures in trapdoor knapsacks*; IEEE Trans. Information Theory, v. IT-24, 1978, pp. 525–530.

[69] R. C. Merkle; *A Fast Software One-Way Hash Function*; Journal of Cryptology, v. 3, n. 2, 1990, pp. 43–58.

[70] R. C. Merkle; *Evaluation of MD4 (as submitted to RIPE*; RIPE Internal Report 1991-5, 1991.

[71] S. Miyaguchi, A. Shiraishi, A. Shimizu; *Fast Data Encryption Algorithm Feal-8*; Review of electrical communications laboratories, v. 36, n. 4, 1988.

[72] S. Miyaguchi, K. Ohta, M. Iwata; *128-bit hash function (N-Hash)*; Proceedings of SECURICOM '90, 1990, pp. 123–137.

[73] V. S. Miller; *Use of Elliptic Curves in Cryptography*; Advances in Cryptology — Proceedings of CRYPTO '85, Springer LNCS 218, 1986, pp. 417–426.

[74] P. Montgomery; *Modular Multiplication without Trial Division*; Math. Comp., v. 44, n. 170, 1985, pp. 519–521.

[75] P. Montgomery; *Speeding the Pollard and elliptic curve methods of factorization*; Math. Comp., v. 48, n. 177, 1987, pp. 243–264.

[76] P. Montgomery, R. Silverman; *An FFT Extension to the $p-1$ Factoring Algorithm*; Math. Comp., v. 54, n. 190, 1990, pp. 839–854.

[77] J. H. Moore; *Protocol Failures in Cryptosystems*; Proceedings of the IEEE, v. 76, n. 5, 1988, pp. 594–602.

[78] M. Naor, M. Yung; *Universal one-way hash functions and their cryptographic applications*; Proceedings of the twenty first annual ACM Symp. Theory of Computing, STOC, 1989, pp. 33–43.

[79] National Institute of Standards and Technology; *Digital signature standard (DSS)*; Federal Information Processing Standards Publication XX, Draft, 1991.

[80] J. Pollard; *Monte Carlo methods for index computation* (mod p); Mathematics of Computation, v. 32, 1978, pp. 918–924.

[81] J.-J. Quisquater; *Announcing the smart card with RSA capability*; Proceedings of the Conference: IC Cards and Applications, Today and Tomorrow, Amsterdam, 1989.

[82] R. L. Rivest, A. Shamir, L. Adleman; *A Method for Obtaining Digital Signatures and Public-Key Cryptosystems*; CACM, v. 21, n. 2, 1978, pp. 120–126.

[83] R. L. Rivest; *The MD4 Message Digest Algorithm*; Abstracts CRYPTO '90, 1990, pp. 281–291.

[84] R. L. Rivest; *MD5 — New Message-Digest Algorithm*; Presented at Rump session of CRYPTO '91, 1991.

[85] J. Rompel; *One-way Functions are Necessary and Sufficient for Secure Signatures*; Proceedings of the twenty second annual ACM Symp. Theory of Computing, STOC, 1990, pp. 387–394.

[86] T. Rosati; *A High Speed Data Encryption Processor for Public Key Cryptography*; Proceedings of the IEEE Custom Integrated Circuits Conference, 1989, pp. 12.3.1–12.3.5.

[87] R. A. Rueppel; *Analysis and Design of Stream Ciphers*; Springer, Berlin, 1986.

[88] A. K. Salomaa; *Formal Languages*; Academic Press, New York, 1973.

[89] A. K. Salomaa; *Public-Key Cryptography*; Springer, 1990.

[90] C. P. Schnorr, H. W. Lenstra, Jr.; *A Monte Carlo factoring algorithm with linear storage*; Math. Comp., v. 43, n. 167, 1984, pp. 289–311.

[91] C. P. Schnorr; *Efficient Identification and Signatures for Smart Cards*; Advances in Cryptology — Proceedings of CRYPTO '89, Springer LNCS 435, 1989, pp. 239–252.

[92] C. P. Schnorr; *An Efficient Cryptographic Hash Function*; Presented at Rump session of CRYPTO '91, 1991.

[93] C. P. Schnorr; *Factoring Integers and Computing Discrete Logarithms via Diophanitne Approximation*; Abstracts of EURO-CRYPT '91, 1991, pp. 141–146.

[94] C. P. Schnorr; *Lattice Basis Reduction: Improved Practical Algorithms and Solving Subset Sum Problems*; to appear in: Proceedings of the FCT' 91, LNCS.

[95] R. Schoof; *Elliptic curves over finite fields and the computation of square roots* (mod p); Mathematics of Computation, v. 44, 1985), pp. 483–494.

[96] A. Shamir; *A polynomial-time algorithm for breaking the basic Merkle-Hellman cryptosystem*; IEEE Trans. Information Theory, v. IT-30, 1984, pp. 699–704.

[97] M. Shand, P. Bertin, J. Vuillemin; *Hardware speedups in long integer multiplication*; Proceedings of the 2nd Annual ACM Symposium on Parallel Algorithms and Architectures, 1990, pp. 138–145.

[98] D. Shanks; *Class Number, A Theory of Factorization and Genera*; Proc. Sympos. Pure Math., v. 20, Amer. Math. Soc. Providence. R I, 1971, pp. 415–440.

[99] A. Shimizu, S. Miyaguchi; *Fast Data Encryption Algorithm Feal*; Advances in Cryptology — Proceedings of EUROCRYPT '87, Springer LNCS 304, 1987, pp. 267–378.

[100] J. H. Silverman; *The Arithmetic of Elliptic Curves*; Springer, New York, 1980.

[101] R. D. Silverman; *The multiple polynomial quadratic sieve*; Math. Comp., v. 48, n. 177, 1987, pp. 329–339.

[102] G. J. Simmons; *Some Number Theoretic Questions Arising in Asymmetric Encryption Techniques*; Annual Meeting of AMS, Biloxi, Mississippi, 1979, AMS Abstract #763.94.1, pp. 136–151.

[103] G. J. Simmons (ed.); *Contemporary Cryptology: The Science of Information Integrity*; IEEE Press, 1991.

[104] J. Van Tilburg; *On the McEliece Cryptosystem*; Advances in Cryptology — Proceedings of CRYPTO '88, Springer LNCS 403, 1988, pp. 119–131.

[105] Yang Yi Xian; *New public-key distribution systems*; Electronics Letters, v. 23, n. 11, 1987, pp. 560–561.

[106] Y. Zheng, T. Matsumoto, H. Imai; *On the Construction of Block Ciphers Provably Secure and Not Relying on Any Unproved Hypotheses*; Advances in Cryptology — Proceedings of CRYPTO '89, Springer LNCS 435, 1989, pp. 461–480.

Lecture Notes in Computer Science

For information about Vols. 1–491
please contact your bookseller or Springer-Verlag